Nature Walks

Beside the Sea

FRANKLIN WATTS
LONDON • SYDNEY

First published in 2010 by
Franklin Watts
338 Euston Road
London NW1 3BH

Franklin Watts Australia
Level 17/207 Kent Street
Sydney NSW 2000

Copyright © 2010 Franklin Watts

ISBN: 978 0 7496 9324 4

Dewey classification number: 577.6'99

A CIP catalogue for this book is available from the British Library.

Planning and production by
Discovery Books Limited
Managing editor: Laura Durman
Editor: Clare Collinson
Picture research: Clare Collinson
Designer: Robert Walster, Big Blu Design

Photographs: FLPA: pp. 15, 17, 18 (D P Wilson), p. 19 (B Borrell Casals), p. 20 (Bob Gibbons), p. 23 (Terry Whittaker), pp. 24t, 25t, 26t (Erica Olsen); istockphoto.com: p. 8 (Margo vanLeeuwen), p. 9 (Ian Hamilton), p. 12 (Stephen Muskie), p. 13 (Alan Crawford), p. 14 (Hans-Martens), p. 16 (Susan McManus), p. 21 (Andrew Helwich), p. 22 (Richard Bowden), p. 25b (Carsten Madsen), p. 27c (Duncan Astbury); Shutterstock Images: title page (Elena Grigorova), p. 6 (Stephen Aaron Rees), p. 7 (Pichugin Dmitry), p. 10 (Ismael Montero Verdu), p. 11 (mtr), p. 24b (TTphoto), p. 26b (Karsten Scherschanski), p. 27t (Jose Gil), p. 27b (Scott Latham), p. 28t (Photoroller), p. 28c (Planner), p. 28b (jamalludin).

Illustrations: istockphoto.com: pp. 7, 9, 14, 16, 20, 22, 26t, 26b (Nick Dinnen), pp. 10, 18 (carduus), pp. 12, 27 (johanna zunino).

Cover images: Shutterstock Images: main (Stephen Aaron Rees), top left (Elena Grigorova), bottom right (Timur Kulgarin).

Printed in China

Franklin Watts is a division of Hachette Children's Books, an Hachette UK company.
www.hachette.co.uk

Seashore safety

When you go for a nature walk by the sea, go with an adult. If you are walking on rocks, wear shoes with a good grip so you do not slip, and do not go into the rock pools.

Contents

Words that appear in **bold** in the text are explained in the glossary.

Seashore wildlife

Let's go for a nature walk by the sea. A seashore **habitat** is good place to discover many kinds of wildlife.

UP CLOSE

The best time to explore the seashore is at **low tide**. This is when the sea covers less of the shore, so you will see more plants and animals.

Did you hear a seagull squawking?
The seashore is home to many kinds of gulls.

Let's see what other types of
wildlife we can find.

Sand dunes and shingle

Let's go up to the **sand dunes**. It's windy here and the sand is very dry.

Marram grass grows well in dry sand. It has long **roots** to soak up water and stems that bend in the wind.

marram grass

This beach is made of shingle. Notice how the stones move under your feet. Strong waves can move the stones, too. Plants that grow here need long, strong roots to hold them in the ground.

sea kale

shingle

9

The sandy shore

Who made these squiggly mounds in the wet sand?

They are **casts**, made by worms as they burrowed tunnels in the sand.

When you walk along a sandy beach, you may think there are no animals living there. Dig down and see what you can find!

When the tide is out, many shellfish hide in the sand.

It's fun to look for empty shells washed up on the shore. See how many kinds you can find.

Seashore birds

Look, there is a bird at the edge of the sea. It has found a worm!

plover

When the tide goes out, you can often see birds such as plovers feeding on worms and shellfish.

Did you hear a cackling call from the cliffs?

gannet

These noisy birds are gannets. They gather together in **colonies** to **breed**.

UP CLOSE

Gannets are excellent divers. They fly down from the high cliffs and plunge into the sea to catch fish.

Onto the rocks

Let's go onto the rocks. This is a good place to find many different plants and animals.

UP CLOSE

Rock pools form on rocky shores when the tide goes out. Pools of water are left behind in the hollows between the rocks.

This **seaweed** feels slimy. Its slimy coating stops it drying out when the tide goes out.

UP CLOSE

The pockets of air in seaweed **fronds** help them to float when they are covered by water – a bit like armbands!

frond

air pocket

Limpets and urchins

These cone-shaped shells are limpets.
Under the shells are the limpets' soft bodies.

UP CLOSE

When the tide is out, limpets clamp themselves tightly to the rocks. When they are covered by water, they move about, feeding on seaweed.

Be careful not to touch these prickly sea urchins at the edge of the rock pool. Their round bodies are covered in **poisonous** spikes.

UP CLOSE

When sea urchins die their spikes fall off, leaving a round skeleton called a test.

In the rock pool

What creatures can we see in the rock pool?

tentacles

These are sea anemones. They look a bit like flowers, but they are a type of animal. They use their poisonous **tentacles** to catch small sea creatures.

Look, there is a crab crawling
out from its hiding place.

UP CLOSE

Crabs have
eight legs, two
large claws and
a hard shell. They often
stay safe by hiding
under stones or
burrowing in
the sand.

shell

leg

claw

leg

19

Fish and starfish

It can be difficult to spot fish in rock pools. They often use **camouflage** to hide from their enemies.

This fish is hiding among the weeds in the rock pool. Can you see it?

Look, there is a starfish.
It has five arms, but no
head! Its mouth is on the
underside of its body.

UP CLOSE

Starfish do
not have heads,
eyes or brains. If
they lose an arm
they can grow
another one.

Watching the sea

Did you hear a barking sound? There is a seal coming out of the sea.

Seals spend most of their time at sea, near to rocky coasts. They come to the shore to breed.

Look further out to sea. There are some dolphins leaping out of the water.

Dolphins often swim in large groups called schools. Look out for them swimming near to boats.

Through the year

The seashore is a good place to look for wildlife all through the year.

Spring

Spring is the season of new life. Look out for baby rabbits and birds' nests in the sand dunes.

Summer

In summer, listen for insects buzzing on the shore and look for wild flowers blooming on the cliffs.

Autumn

In autumn, the weather can be wet and windy. This is a good time to go **beachcombing**. Autumn storms wash many exciting things onto the shore.

Winter

Winter is a good time to spot birds on the seashore. Some birds visit for the winter from colder countries.

25

Be a nature detective

When you go for a nature walk by the sea, be a nature detective and look for these things:

Seal tracks in the sand

If you see tracks in the sand, their size and shape will give you a clue about the animal that has made them. Follow the tracks and see what you find!

Sea urchin test

If you find a sea urchin test on the shore, you will see it is covered in bumps. The bumps are where the urchin's spikes were when it was alive.

Hermit crab

If you see a shell moving on the sand, it may not be quite what it seems. Hermit crabs do not have shells of their own. They live inside the empty shells of other sea animals.

Empty egg cases

Look among the seaweed washed up on the shore. You may find a spongy ball that once contained a sea creature's eggs.

Fossils

The seashore is a good place to find **fossils**. Fossils give you clues about the plants and animals that lived millions of years ago.

Nature walk tips

If at first you do not see any animals on the shore, keep looking. Dig down in the sand, look under seaweed and lift stones, but be careful not to harm the animals you see. If you do move something to look underneath, always put it back where you found it. It is important not to touch eggs in nests or pick wild flowers.

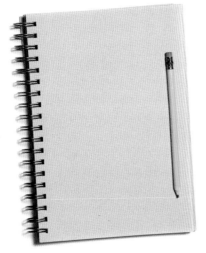

Put a notepad and pencil in a plastic bag and take it with you. Make notes about the animals and plants you find or draw sketches of them. Then you can learn more about them at home or at school.

If you have a camera, take it with you so you can photograph the animals and plants you see.

Binoculars will help you spot birds on the cliffs or out at sea.

Remember, do not go exploring alone and take extra care when walking on rocks.

Glossary

beachcombing searching the seashore for things washed up by the sea

breed to produce young by mating

camouflage a way of hiding by blending in with the surroundings

cast a mound of sand or mud left on the surface by a burrowing worm

colonies large numbers of the same kind of animal living closely together

fossil the remains of an animal or plant preserved in rock

fronds the leaves of plants such as seaweed and ferns

habitat the home of a group of animals and plants

low tide the lowest point that the water reaches on the shore when the surface of the sea moves with the tides

poisonous able to cause illness or death by producing a harmful substance

roots the parts of a plant that grow down into the ground

sand dune a mound or ridge of sand formed by the wind

seaweed a plant that grows in the sea or on rocks

tentacles long, thin parts of an animal that are used to catch food

Index